I See a Child

Learning About Learning Educational Foundation is a non-profit corporation dedicated to the development of materials and projects which use the creative process as the basis for the education of children.

In the past twenty years Learning About Learning has involved over 40,000 children and educators in the discovery and development of their human resources. Its credits range from community development projects to educational foreign exchange programs. Learning About Learning has recently made its activities, projects and ideas available to the general public in written and audio-visual form.

Cindy Herbert participated in Learning About Learning's incipient creative arts programs as a child and taught other children while still in high school. At Trinity University she studied drama under Paul Baker and she has directed many creative arts programs. She is presently a principal writer for the Learning About Learning Educational Foundation.

I See a Child

by Cindy Herbert

Anchor Books
Anchor Press/Doubleday & Company, Inc.
Garden City, New York

The Learning About Learning Educational Foundation
Series: 1

Anchor Books Edition: 1974

ISBN: 0-385-04158-6
Library of Congress Catalog Card Number 72-96280
Copyright © Learning About Learning, 1973
All Rights Reserved
Printed in the United States of America

First Edition

TO KIM

ACKNOWLEDGMENTS

I wish to acknowledge a debt of gratitude:
To Paul Baker, Director, Trinity University Drama Department and the Dallas Theater Center, whose selfless respect for and active development of the individuals's creative life is a standard for us all; Paul Kantz, Associate Superintendent, San Antonio Independent School District, for his empathetic and active support; to Joyce Sowells, principal of Milam Elementary School, for her sustaining humanitarian spirit; to the following children and students some of whose photographs appear in this book; and to all the children, who taught us more than we taught them: Mary Frances Beavers, Bertine Branch, Joshua Cantrell, Ruth Cantrell, Henry Castillo, Robyn Cloughley, Lisa Cook, Aida Coy, Arlene Ellison, Darlene Ellison, Gregory Hinojosa, Kelly Jarrell, Rod Katts, Peggy Kokernot, Jeffrey Leon, Missy Light, Cathy Liu, Cynthia Martinez, Michael Martinez, Valerie Mayfield, Helen McCaffrey, Sarah McLinden, Robert Medrano, Robert Mora, Mimi Norton, Sevy Norton, Kim Ridgeway, Cory Russell, Beatrice Valdez, Gilbert Valdez, Catherine Yoes, Gregory Young; to Marie Brown and Ronnie Shushan of Doubleday & Company for their straightforward and understanding criticism in the preparation of this book; to the following for inspiration, assistance and countless contributions: Nellie Amido, Sieglinde Bayol, Johnny Gutierrez, Meg Hathaway, David Herbert, John Herbert, Charles Jarrell, Julia Jarrell, Helen Martinsen, Susan Russell, Gonzalo Torres, Cha Cha Ximenes, Deck Yoes; and especially to Jearnine Wagner, Director, Learning About Learning Educational Foundation, my friend and mentor.

Design: Susan Russell
Photography: John Herbert

C. H.

I See a Child

I SEE A CHILD

I see a child
I see him happy, sad, worried, angry, indifferent.

I try to be nice.
I try to be understanding.

And he makes me laugh.
He makes me cry.
He disappoints me.
He takes advantage.

I try to see him as he is but sometimes I react without listening.

How can I put aside my own feelings long enough to see through his eyes?
To understand his point of view?

How much of what I see in this child is colored by my own expectations?

How can I see beyond the obvious?

The relationship that develops between the teacher and student forms a foundation for what is taught and learned in the classroom. What I see in a child will strongly affect the kind of relationship that forms.

A positive relationship takes conscious work to see the other person as he truly is. At first most of the work must come from me, the teacher.

My responsibility is not as easy as it seems: I must become interested in another human being.

At first I see the children that I teach through the filters of my own experience. My upbringing, my background, my education all help me to form a mental picture of children. Before I enter the classroom, I have strong expectations about the students I will encounter.

YOU DON'T KNOW ME

You have me pegged before I walk in the door.
You look at my grades
My aptitude tests
My I.Q.
You talk to other teachers about me and my sisters and brothers
And you have me pegged before I step in the door.
How could I ever change your mind?

ate roles create expectations create roles create expectations create roles creat

ns create roles create expectations create roles creat

s create expectations create roles create

e expectations create roles create

ctations create roles creat

ions create roles create

s create roles create

eate roles create

te roles create

les create

expectations create roles create expectations create roles create expectations cr

expectations create roles create expectations create r

expectations create roles create expecta

expectations create roles create e

expectations create roles cr

expectations create role

expectations create

expectations crea

expectations c

expectatio

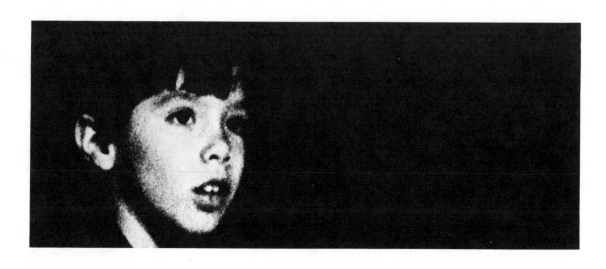

EXPECTATIONS

Held back a grade ... Dumb ... I.Q. 85 ... Poor Achiever ... Slow Learner.

EXPECTATIONS

Scream!! Run wild!! Yell!!

EXPECTATIONS
We love you, ma'am.

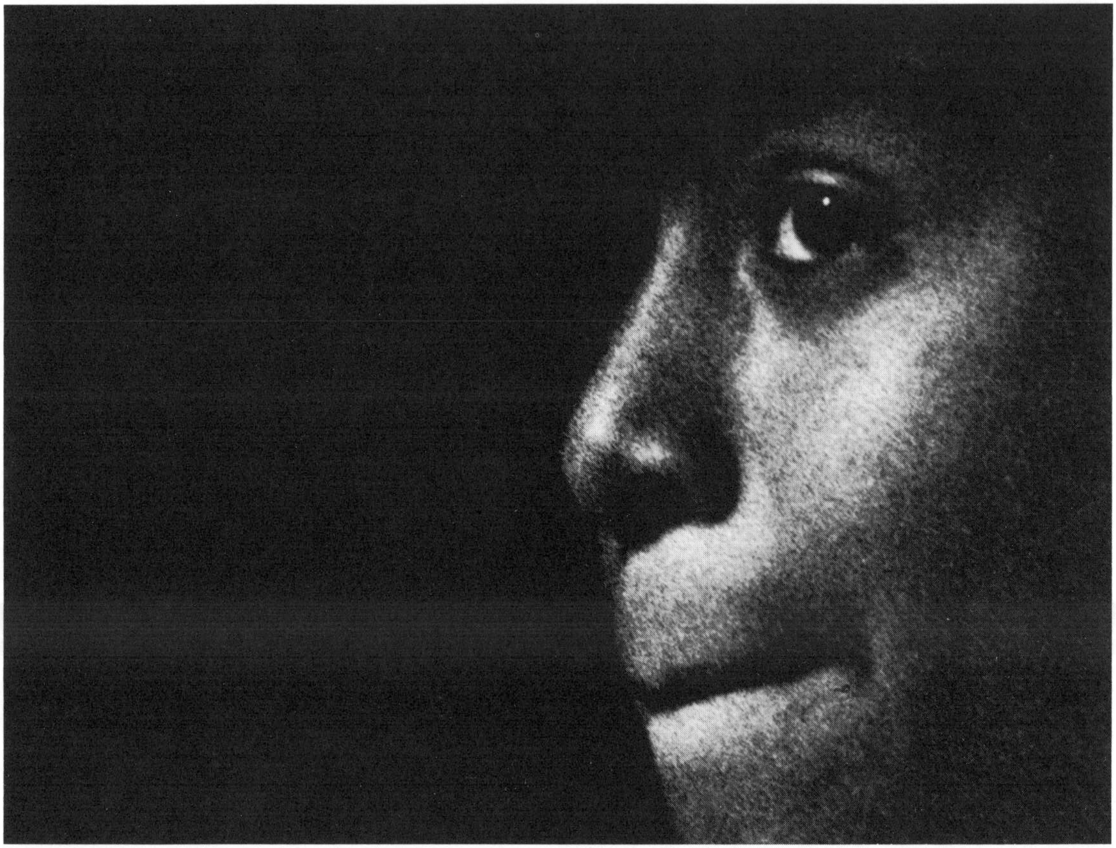

EXPECTATIONS

starestarestarestarestarestarestarestarestarestarestarestarestarestar

Guided by my expectations, I plan how I will behave when I enter the classroom.
I plan how I will present myself to the children.

I am expected to do a good job.
I want to do a good job.
My idea of doing a good job is behaving like the image of what a good
teacher should be.

All the children loved Miss Soulful. She was so beautiful and so sweet. When she read stories they looked at her with adoring eyes. They realized that she really wanted to "do" something for them. She wanted the children to love her so she never gave bad marks. She never realized how the children took advantage of her.

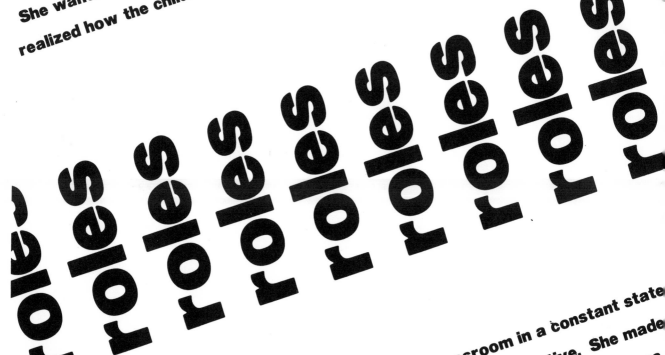

Miss Vigor always came on strong and kept her classroom in a constant state of excitement. She wanted the children to be creative. She made beautiful lesson plans but the class didn't always do what she expected. She concluded that children had no sense of appreciation.

Once there was
a teacher who did
everything by the book. The children
she taught were all polite and well-mannered. The
principal loved her because she had the neatest and quietest
room in the whole school. Her room became a showplace for visitors; but
the children acted differently when school was out.

roles roles roles roles roles roles roles roles

If anyone asked
a question that Mr. Narcissum couldn't answer, he'd make them
give a report on it the next day. All the children were
awed and impressed by his vast knowledge,
and they wished they could
memorize as well as
he could.

What kind of role will I play?
Will I be a drill sergeant?
Will I be a pollyanna?
Will I be a pushover?
Will I be a nag?
What kind of role will I play?

To play a role I find I must hide behind a mask of authority or kindness or intelligence.
The role shows only one side of me. It conceals my multi-dimensional individuality.

I present myself to the children as a role, not a person.
Instead of being myself, I act the part of a teacher.

The children see and respond to my role, not me.

They respond by playing roles themselves. My behavior tells them what role to play.

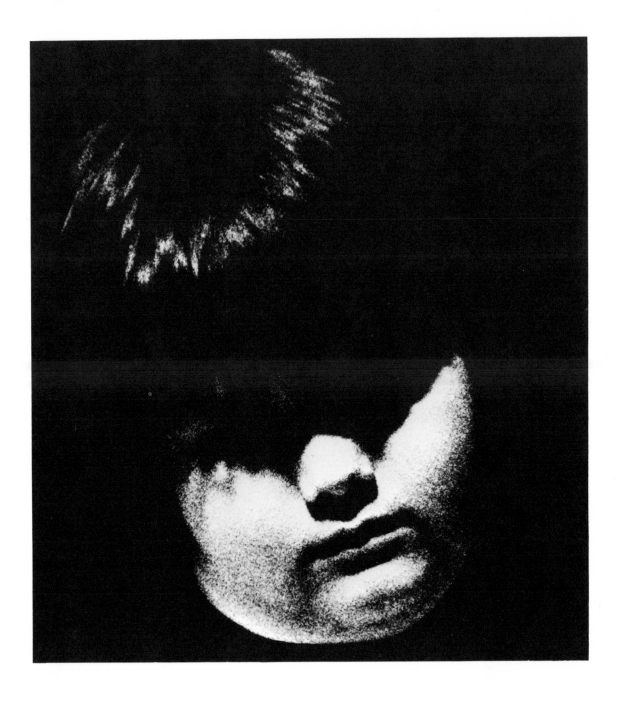

THE MONSTER

You're afraid of me!
I throw things.
I hit people.
You pretend not to see.
I talk back and you do nothing.
You never tell me what I should or shouldn't do
Except in the most polite way.
You're afraid of me
And I'm scared.
Who knows what you might let me do?
Please, please tell me when to stop—
Don't be afraid of me!

I don't see the reality of the children.
I only see their roles.
And their roles demand a response from me.
Since I am determined to stay in control of the situation, I counter their roles
by acting even tougher, smarter, or nicer in my chosen role.

It isn't very satisfying playing a role instead of being myself.
The children and I are acting out a frustrating drama of roles and counter-roles.
The predictability of our responses in these roles interferes with my
teaching and their learning. I wish I could break the cycle and begin anew.

THE PERFORMER

I'll do anything to make you see me.
I want you to like me.
I really get your attention when I do funny things.
Someday maybe I could share with you the quiet side of me.
I wonder if you would notice me like that?

My expectations start this unsatisfying game I'm playing.
Before I even meet the children I make up my mind what they will be like.
Instead of responding to the children as individual human beings, I am respond-
ing to an image of children that is in my head.

Each time I expect a child to be dumb, he responds by acting dumb.
He protects himself by acting as I expect him to act.

TEACHER'S PET

What do you want in return for your favors?
What do you want of me?
When I smile you seem to melt.
I like to be important to you
But
I want the other kids to like me, too.
Shall I go on smiling and acting sweet?
Is that what you want?

What do I expect to see?
Do I have the courage to let go of my expectations?

A real person is not one-dimensional.

The dumb children, the smart children, the mean ones, the sweet ones are all in my head, not in my classroom.

To form a positive relationship with a child I must look beneath his surface facade and seek out his other dimensions.

LOOK LOOK

listen

question

listen

question

listen

question

listen

question

listen

listen
question
listen
question
listen
question
listen
question
listen

LOOK LOOK

How does he dress?
Is he healthy?
Is he of a different ethnic group?
Is he fatter, skinnier, prettier, uglier, stronger, weaker, taller, or shorter than the others?
How does he use words?
What does he keep in his pockets?
What does he eat for lunch?
How do I judge his appearance?
How does my judgment affect my behavior toward him?

This time I try to push aside all expectations of how I will behave, how the children will behave and what will happen in the classroom.
My goal is to see what the children really look like and to listen to what they really sound like. I want to form a real picture of real people.

I look.
I listen.

What is he doing just to please me?
What is he doing just to bother me?
How does he feel about me?
     does he have a crush?
     is he afraid?
     does he act superior?
     does he hit me?
     does he ignore me?
     does he hold my hand?
     does he continually test me?
     does he listen to me?
     does he understand me?
How does he think he is supposed to relate to teachers? adults?
What does he want or need from our relationship?

What does he think I feel about him?

My role playing is not the only reason the children play roles. They continue even when I stop. Before I ever met them they learned ways of responding to grown-ups.

I wonder how past interactions have shaped, changed and influenced the children I see.

Everyone and everything in his world tells a child what to think, what to do, and what to be. Parents, friends, television, the larger society, all have their say. They all have roles for him, goals for him to reach, images for him to maintain.

The child is in the center of all these voices and pressures struggling to make sense of the world, to find his place, to discover his identity, to make his mark on things.

Keep your promises.

Respect your family.

To get a good job, get a good education.

Make peace, not war.

Learn to be satisfied with what you are.

Children should be seen and not heard.

If you work hard enough, you can reach any goal.

Once you make up your mind, stick to it!

Always be honest.

Live your life to the fullest.

An unmarried person is only half a person.

Beauty is only skin deep.

Smile!

Be open about your feelings.

If you want people to like you, you must be a good
listener.

Never purposely hurt anyone else.

Money isn't everything.

Promise anything to get what you want.
Parents don't know how you really feel.
School is a bummer!
Don't be a chicken.
The popular kids have all the fun.
What's the matter? Cat got your tongue?
I work hard all my life and my children are still hungry.
The trouble with this world is all the people who are
afraid to change.
Keep your business to yourself.
A man must live up to his responsibilities.
Marriage is a prison.
It gives you sex appeal!
Don't be a phony.
Control yourself!
Don't let anyone jive you!
Hit or get hit!
It's as easy to marry a rich man as a poor man.

TEACHER KNOWS BEST

You say I'm wrong and you're right.
You say I didn't mean it when I did.
You say I wasn't thinking when I was.
You say I'm not myself when I am.

Don't I have a right to judge for myself?

What is MY vision
of what the child should be?
What is the child's vision
of what he should be?

Am I pressuring the child, too?
Am I trying to force my values, my standards, my opinions?

How can I keep my values, let him keep his values, and still like him?

THE BROKEN CLOCK

I have learned a lot today.
I have learned that children are not as important as things
And that children should not break things.
I have learned that accidents aren't really accidents.
There's always someone to blame.

WALKING TO SCHOOL

I'm late again.
I'm late.
And you don't care why.
"Tardiness is
unforgivable," you say.
I'm sick inside and
frightened of your eyes.
I'm late again
And you'll never
let me forget it.
I'm late.
I'm late.
I'm late.
I'm late.
I'm always late to school.

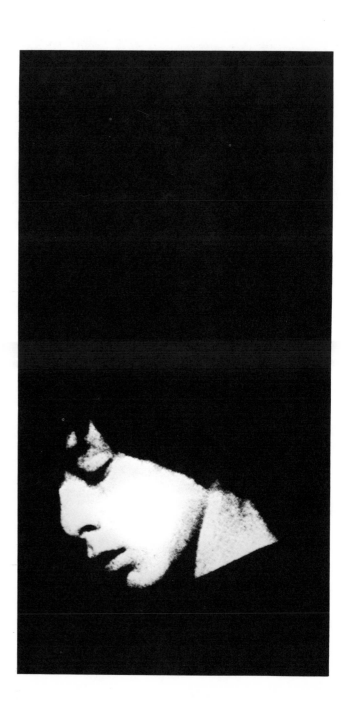

How do I know what the child is really feeling?
How do I know when he's afraid? bored? tired? responsive?
Do I look for reasons behind his actions?
Do I look for reasons that may not be obvious?

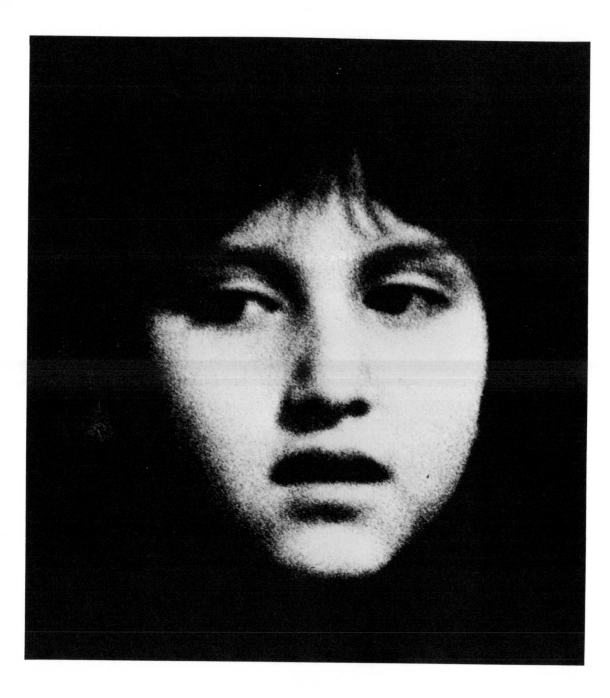

I'M SORRY

When something is missing
When something is broken
I get the blame
It seems as if I'm always blamed
So I
Apologize—
Feeling angry
And humiliated
But not a bit
Sorry.

The pressures on the child push him into a corner.
He is afraid to be himself. He lessens his anxiety by adopting roles. If a child
was told in the past that he is dumb, he will expect me to also think
him dumb and to treat him accordingly. So he salvages a little of his
identity by calling himself dumb before I can.

THE THEFT

Everyone knows I took your money.
I don't show it and they don't show it.
But everyone knows I did it.
THIEF.
All I wanted was a little money to buy a ring.
I didn't know it would make me a thief.

There is more to a child than the roles he has learned.

I look at the child.
I listen to the child.
This time I go outside of the school situation. I find out as much as I can about each child and the everyday life he leads when he's not in school.

Family

Where does the child live?
Who are the people in his family?
What is his role in his family?
Are there special problems in his home?
Are there pressures from home that I don't know about?

How do his parents feel about school?
Does he have a space of his own at home?
Does he act the same way at home as he does at school?
Have I ever visited his home and community?

Friends

What does this child like to play? where? with whom?
Do other children like him?
Is he a leader? a loner?
What does he talk about with his friends?
What do they like to do?
What does his group think is cool?
What role does he play in his group?
Does he listen to his friends more than to anyone else?
Do I ever force him to choose between my values and his friends' values?
What behavior gives him status in school?
What behavior gives him status in his group?
Is there a difference?

IN MY FAMILY

We listen with our eyes down.
When we really listen
We listen with our eyes down
So don't think
I'm dumb or shy or disrespectful
I just learned to listen with my eyes
Cast down.

A SENSE OF HUMOR

Thank goodness my mother has a sense of humor.
Sometimes she gets tired of the noise
And blows her top.
(She can really give it to you when she's mad)
But if I can tease her in a gentle way
To get her to see my side
She'll laugh out loud and let go of her anger.
Then
If I keep the noise down
She'll keep her humor up.

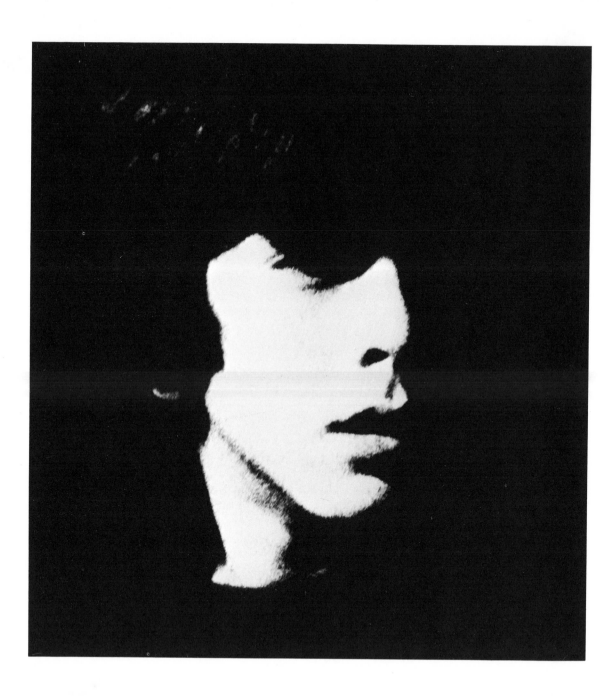

PEOPLE AREN'T ALWAYS WHAT THEY SEEM

My little brother pulls on my hair
But he really just wants me to play

My big sister yells when she helps me dress
But she really just wants me to look good

My big brother is always nosey when I go somewhere
But he really just wants to protect me

My aunt complains when my grades aren't good
But she really just wants me to do well in life

My parents are never satisfied no matter what I do
But I know they want me to live a better life than theirs

My family makes me angry and I fuss a lot
But I really know I'm wanted and I'm loved.

MY FATHER

I wish all adults would behave
Like my father does.
He demands that we be quiet and listen.
He doesn't yell.
He doesn't act sweet.
He just clearly tells me what to do.
Please demand the same things of me—
It helps me to control myself.

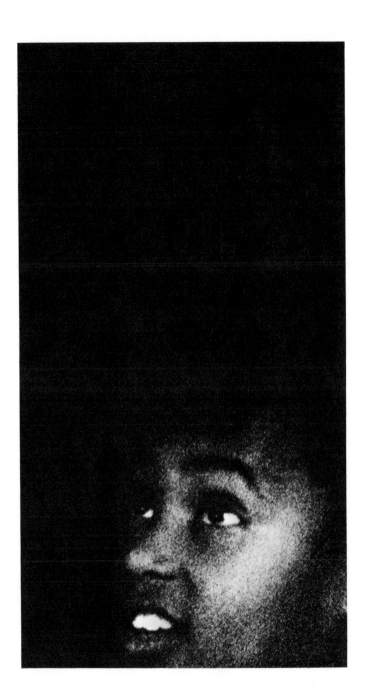

In the classroom I get but a glimpse of what each child can do, make, be. He has a larger life away from me.

If the child comes from a cultural heritage that is different from my own, I may know little or nothing of the history of relationships, traditions, and values that have helped to shape the child.

To understand more about him, I ask him questions about himself, his family and his friends. I ask him to respond to my questions in new ways.
I ask him to write, draw, pantomime, tell stories and create plays.

How do people do things in his neighborhood?
How do they communicate?
What do they cherish and celebrate?
What are special events to them?
What is their system of values?
Where do they visit and congregate?
What stories do they tell?
What do they pass down to their children?

Besides classroom activities
I visit his home, his community center, the special meeting places in his
community. I find new ways to talk to him. I see him responding
to others in new ways. I learn a lot more about him.

MY FAMILY

We yell at each other a lot.
We fight.
We complain.
We don't always get along.
But just let an outsider pick on one of us
And we're a team—
Tough, hard,
Working together.

I take part in some of the activities that the child is involved with day after day. I begin to see what his everyday life is like. I get to know him and his family in their own territory.

And I find a lot of surprises there.
I discover some of the riches in his background.

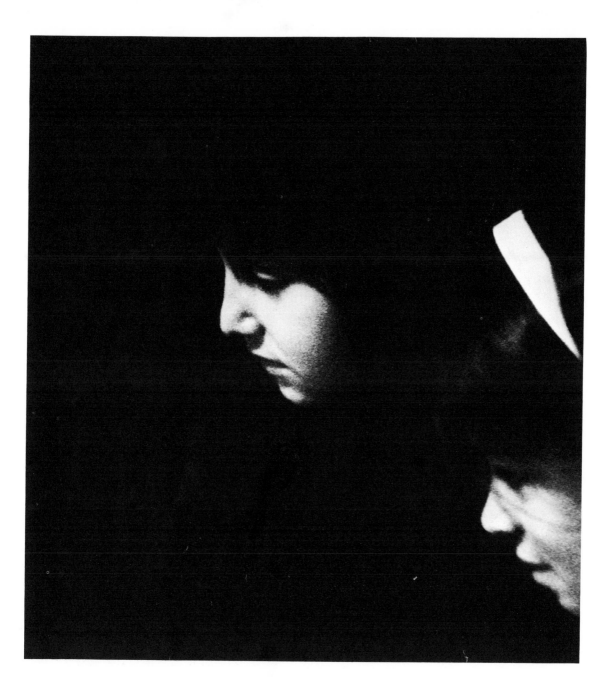

He comes from a unique heritage with its own traditions and rituals.
Every day he encounters people, places, objects, sights, sounds and smells
That are an incredible resource for feelings and ideas.

He already knows about enough people to fill a dozen novels.
He already asks enough questions to begin a hundred scientific experiments.
He already has enough experiences to write an historical chronicle.
He already possesses enough memories for a lifetime of ideas, creations and inventions.

Before I can teach him anything, I must know something about what he has already learned.

His everyday world may pressure and pull him, but it also strengthens his sense of identity, of value, of worth.

What turns him off?
What turns him on?
What is important to him?
What is beautiful? terrible? embarrassing?
What is he shy about?
What is masculine to him? feminine?
What does he think is cool? tough? fun?
What would he like to do? to be?
What are his dreams about himself?

A child comes to me, not as an empty vessel to be filled, but already full of experiences, values and abilities. In his short life he has already solved a lot of problems, thought a lot of thoughts, tried out a lot of ideas. That is where I must begin with a child: with what he already is.

What he is will be different from what I am. I may not like what he is. I may think his family didn't bring him up the way I would have. But if I wish to communicate with this child, to open new worlds to him, I must begin where he is.

LEARNING ABOUT ME

**I'm learning a lot with you, teacher
I'm learning what it means to be myself.**

I return to the classroom full of new information and fresh expectations.

In the course of a day I watch what happens to a child when he is not expected to be a bully or to be the smart one or the dumb one. I see what happens when he is expected simply to respond, to express his feelings, his dreams, his wonderings, his ideas.

Given a chance to be the best he is, the child responds by becoming alive, Our relationship really becomes a relationship and he is free to become interested in me.

I begin to look for the most meaningful part of myself that I can share with him.

me me me me me me

me me me me me me

WHAT CAN I DO?

me me me me me me

me me me me me me

WHAT CAN I DO?

me me me me me me

me me me me me me

WHAT CAN I DO?

e me me me me m
e me me me me m
me WHAT CAN I DO?
e me me me me m
e me me me me m
me WHAT CAN I DO?
e me me me me m
e me me me me m
WHAT CAN I DO?

To get to know myself a little better I collect memories from the past. I ask questions about myself — the same questions I ask about a child.

What is my background? my heritage?
How was I brought up?
What was I taught to be?
What was I taught to value?
What did I do when my time was my own?
What did I think about? wonder?
What did I want to be?
What did I create for myself?

Memories of School

The room was big and smelled of chalk and old books . . .
I remember the wood of the desk and chair . . .
Outside was a big oak tree we used to climb after school . . .
My teacher was tall and she wore purple dresses . . .
Once I had to stay in during recess when I was caught chewing gum . . .
My birthday party was celebrated on the playground . . .
One time I got "needs to improve" in "gets along well with others . . ."
Getting chosen for the baseball team was an awful experience . . .
My parents expected me to make "A's" of course . . .
When did I decide to become a teacher? It's hard to remember . . .

I forget a lot of the joys and fears — the zest for living — the innocence of being a child.
As I come into touch with the child I used to be, I find it easier to come into touch with the children in my classroom.
I share the me of the past with my children.
I share with them the me of the present.

TELL ME A STORY

Tell me about when you were
    my age.
Tell me about your family and
    your friends.
Tell me what you did all day
    when you were a kid.
Tell me again about that time
    you got in trouble
And didn't know why.
I'm so relieved to know you
    used to be a kid, too.

My memories accumulate in a scrapbook. It is a rich resource from which to draw
ideas and feelings; from which to share experiences with the children.

EMPATHY

When things go wrong
I can remember,
Word for word,
Everything you said to me,
Everything you did to me,
And I can remember,
Clear as day
Just how I felt.
But what did you feel?
What did I do?
I haven't the slightest idea.
I wonder why?

How can I see my own behavior toward a child as clearly as I see his behavior toward me?
I want our relationship to deepen.
Even in the happiest relationships things sometimes go wrong and no one knows why or what to do about it.

CUSS WORDS

I said those things
To get a reaction,
But you didn't do
What you usually do.
You didn't look shocked.
You didn't shout.
You didn't smile.
You didn't quiver.
You simply said,
"I do not like those words.
They will not be heard in my
classroom."
You didn't even tell me I was
bad.
There's a lot more to you
Than I thought.

Everyday I write what I can recall about the behavior that takes place
in the classroom: what is done and said by the children and what is done
and said
by me.

How do I behave?
How does the child behave?
How do we interact with each other?
I collect my everyday observations into a diary. When things go wrong, I
read what I have written and re-evaluate what happened. I look for interaction
patterns that might be forming without my knowledge. I take steps to break
my negative patterns by changing my own behavior.

What is the pattern of our relationship?
Do I ever slander him when all I wanted was to state my position?
Do I ever give in to him when I need to draw the line?
Do I ever let him know what I expect of him?
Do I ever let him know the behavior limits in my classroom?
Do my limits make sense?
Do I ever take advantage of the authority I have over him?

I cannot actually change the behavior of the child.
I can review my own actions and improve upon them.

What do I do that I can change for the better?

My diary gives me an easy way to review the conflicts in our relationship and change what I can for the better.

SAMENESSES

Supposing we had something in common.
Supposing we liked the same thing—
A sunny day,
A sport,
Wind blowing through
The trees.
    Supposing we laughed together.
Do you suppose we might?

BRIDGING THE GAP

We don't exactly speak
The same language.
Our age is different—our thinking is different.
And
We don't use the same words.
But,
Since you let me talk my way,
I'll let you talk your way.
We might just
(Accidentally)
Communicate.

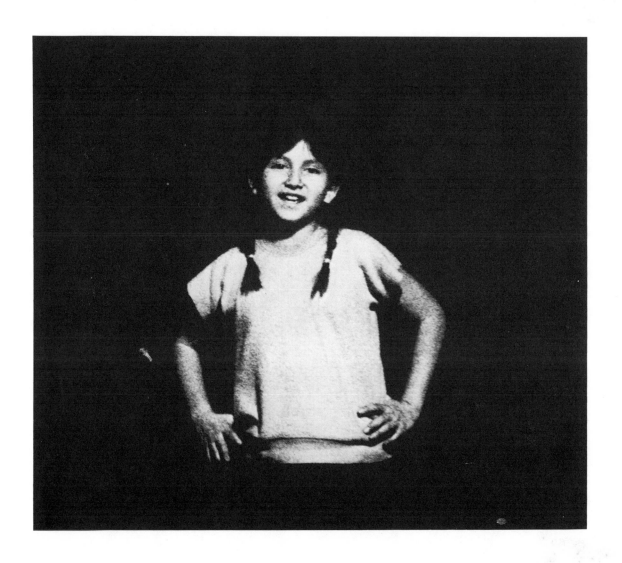

How many ways can two people talk?
What shall we talk about?
What are the best places to talk?
What do I do if the other person doesn't repond?
Could we talk to each other without using words?

YOU SURPRISED ME!

**Today you made a mistake—
And you laughed.
(It was a nice, deep laugh.)
I didn't know teachers
Ever did anything
Silly or funny or
Embarrassing.
I think you're more than just
A teacher—
You're a real person!**

I find every opportunity I can to communicate with this child — not just in the classroom, but in the lunchroom, on the playground, and especially in the child's own neighborhood.

I try to hear what a child is really saying to me.
It takes a special kind of listening to do that. It means I must listen to the person beneath the role. It means I must suspend my initial reactions and give myself a chance to really hear what is happening.

THE QUIET ONE

You probably don't think
I'm listening.
But I am.
I'd be too embarrassed to tell you,
But I hear you.
Please don't turn away from me.
I really am
Listening.

For a long time the child may not want to talk to me at all, no matter how hard I try.

But I don't stop trying. I talk about myself, my family, my memories, I talk about things I do when I'm not in school. I talk about the things that interest and excite me. I show the child that I am curious about my world.

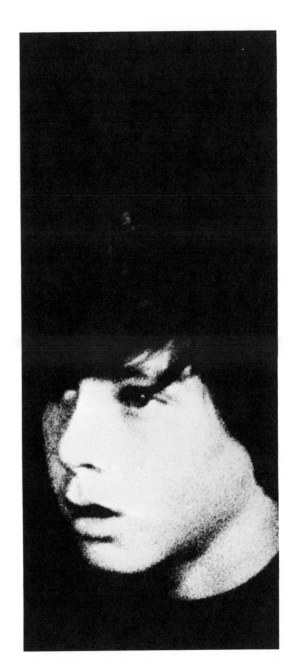

ASK A STUPID QUESTION

You don't make fun of me
like some grown-ups do.
I know some of the things I
worry about are silly;
That my fears don't make
sense.
But those things are real to me.
I'm glad you don't tell me
they're dumb.

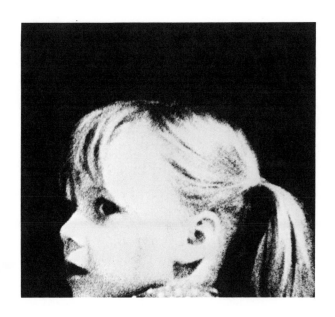

GIMMEE

**I don't always want what
    I ask for.
If I ask for a dime, I might
    be happier with a hug.**

What does he want me to say to him?
What do I want him to say to me?
What do I want to say to him?
Can I take what he says as seriously as he does?

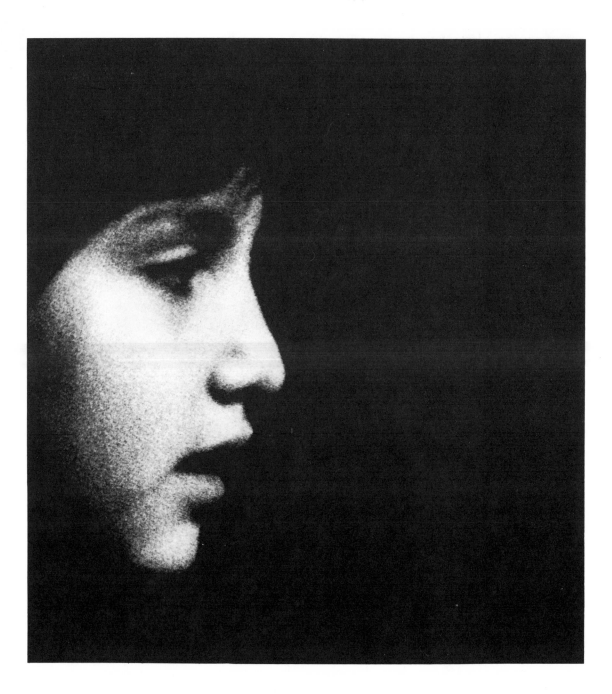

A CONVERSATION

When you and I are talking together,
I hear your words,
I hear the sound of your voice.
I see your eyes thinking, questioning, understanding.
I see the way you sit and stand and move.
I think about what you say.
I wonder if you are saying what you mean.
I wonder what you want me to say to you.
When you and I are talking together,
I see,
I hear,
I think,
Much more than I could ever tell you.

Conversations are deeper than words.
The more we communicate, the more fully I come to know the child as he truly is.

I SEE A CHILD I SEE A C
A CHILD I SEE A CHILD
I SEE A CHILD I SEE A C
A CHILD I SEE A CHILD
I SEE A CHILD I SEE A C
A CHILD I SEE A CHILD
I SEE A CHILD I SEE A C
A CHILD I SEE A CHILD
I SEE A CHILD I SEE A C
A CHILD I SEE A CHILD

I SEE A CHILD I SEE A C
I SEE A CHILD I SEE A CHILD
I SEE A CHILD I SEE A C
I SEE A CHILD I SEE A CHILD
SEE A CHILD I SEE A C
I SEE A CHILD I SEE A CHILD
SEE A CHILD I SEE A C
I SEE A CHILD I SEE A CHILD
SEE A CHILD I SEE A C
I SEE A CHILD I SEE A CHILD

WHAT DOES HE DO?

Does he like to work with his hands?
Does he like to work slowly or quickly?
Does he organize his materials neatly?
Does he spread them all out?
Does he like a variety of materials and problems?
Does he handle things one at a time?
Does he approach work hesitantly or does he dive right in?
How does he think about a problem?
Does he need to talk? sit quietly? draw? write? move around? build?
    act things out?
What does he choose to do when his time is his own?

CONCENTRATION

**I don't care about boring things.
I care about pitching rocks.
Sometimes me and my friend
     spend 3 hours or so
Chunking at a stop sign.
Ping!
Ping!
I can really make it sound.
The secret to rock chunking
Is
Practice
And concentration—
Ping!**

I gain new visions of a child by watching him operate in his everyday world,
by
remembering the child I used to be, by investigating the patterns in our
relationship, by working hard to communicate with him.

When I return to the classroom I see things about the child I had not seen
before.

BUSY WORK

My hands long to be busy
But not with busy work
My mind longs to be busy
But not with busy work
My hands want to stretch
Twist
Mold
My mind wants to run, leap, dance
Busy work
Busy work
I want to fly
Write it again
Write it again
I want to make—to be
Wrong
Do it over
Wrong
Busy work
Busy work
Busy work

What catches his ear?
What catches his eye?
How does he move?
How does he use his hands?
What sounds does he make?

SITTING IN A TREE

This is where I'm happiest—
Swinging
Climbing
Making up stories
Letting my muscles teach me about my world.
I open my eyes and ears
To the wonders
Inside me and
Around me.
Here I think my best ideas.
Imagine my greatest inventions.
Here I feel alive
And full,
I feel like me.

I see that each child is a changing, evolving human being.
He has his own unique way of seeing his world and responding to what is there.
I must form a relationship with the child as a thinker, a mover, a creator.

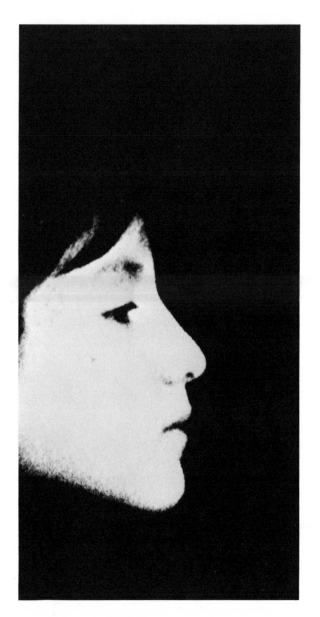

SIT STILL AND LISTEN

You shame me,
Threaten me,
Bribe me
Into motionlessness.
My limbs freeze.
I am a stone.
A stone in a room full of stones
Waiting to be taught.
And you,
The teacher,
Slowly stretch out the moments
Till the bell,
Whereupon
We all
(even you)
Sigh the relief.

A PUSH IN THE RIGHT DIRECTION

I'm a mover
I am movement
I move over, out, in, through, under and around.
I have enough energy and resources
To change my world.
Give me a chance to use what I have.
Give me a little push in the right direction.

I want my classroom to be a place where a child's natural energy and curiosity is directed, not stifled.
I want my classroom to be a place where the differences in
people are exciting and where different minds can learn and grow together.

All these things I want cannot happen overnight, but I have made a small beginning.

I WANT TO KNOW WHY

I want to know how my world
    got to be the way it is
I want to know about people
Places
Ideas.
I want to know how
    things work.
I want to know what causes
    what and
How things fit together.
Most of all—
I want to know
What I can do
Right now
Not when I'm grown
Or rich
Or somewhere else,
But
What can I do NOW
For me
For you
And for our world?

This is the part of the child I become most interested in . . . the part of him that wonders, that asks questions, that responds uniquely to his world.
I want to see that part of him grow. I want to see him use that part of him to create and invent something of value for himself and his world. Little by little I find my own standard for forming a relationship with a
child. I see the potential for growth and development through our experiences together.

LEARNING

Me learning about you.
You learning about me.
Us learning about learning.

Looking beyond the obvious, beyond the surface layer of roles and labels, I discover a whole new and exciting person in each of my students. My world is enriched in ways beyond value.

The children have the most valuable thing that I can give them: an honest, working relationship which demands that we accept each other for what we are.

All our learning is founded on our growth and interactions as multi-dimensional, ever-changing human beings.